# Thor Heyerdahl

## Courage Under Fire

Sofwest Press
Las Cruces, NM, USA

LIVES WORTH LIVING

# Thor Heyerdahl

## Courage Under Fire

by

Colin Evans

*The* Lives Worth Living *Series consists of biographies of men and women whose lives illustrate one or more primary virtues or aspects of good character. The books are written for the young reader in middle school or junior high and include critical thinking questions, a summary chapter, and afterword to parents. The facts and events recorded in this book are true and based upon the most reliable research sources available. However, the author has dramatized some scenes and dialogue to make the text more readable. In such cases, every effort was made to build the dialogue on a foundation of the known facts and the character of the subject.*

*Produced by New England Publishing Associates, Inc. for SOFSOURCE, Inc.*

**Series Editor:** Edward W. Knappman
**Copy Editing:** Miccinello Associates
**Design and Page Composition:** Ron Formica and Christopher Ceplenski
**Photo Researcher:** Victoria Harlow
**Editorial Administration:** Ron Formica and Christopher Ceplenski
**Proofreading:** Doris Troy

**Cover Design:** Gabriel Quesada
**Cover Photo:** Organ Mountains at Sunrise, Las Cruces, NM; Frank Parish

ISBN 1-57163-602-1

Library of Congress Catalog Card Number: 98-84789
Printed in the United States of America
01 00 99 98                    9 8 7 6 5 4 3 2 1

# Table of Contents

# Timeline

| Biographical Milestone | Year | Historical Milestone |
|---|---|---|
| | **1910** | |
| **Oct. 6, 1914:** Thor Heyerdahl is born in Larvik, Norway. | | **Aug. 4, 1914:** Outbreak of First World War. |
| | | **Nov. 1918:** First World War ends. |
| | **1925** | |
| | | **Oct. 1929:** Stock market crashes, sparking the Great Depression. |
| **Sept. 1933:** Thor enrolls at the University of Oslo. | | |
| **Dec. 24, 1936:** Thor marries Liv Torp. | | |
| **Mar. 1938:** Thor and Liv return to Norway. **Oct. 1938:** Thor and Liv move to Canada. | | **Sept. 1, 1939:** Germany invades Poland, signaling the outbreak of World War II. |
| **1940:** Thor joins "Little Norway," the Free Norwegian Forces. | **1940** | |
| | | **Sept. 1945:** World War II ends. |
| **Apr. 28, 1947:** *Kon-Tiki* sets sail from Callao, Peru. **August 7, 1947:** After sailing 4,300 miles in 101 days, *Kon-Tiki* reaches eastern Polynesia. | | |
| **1950:** Publication of *The Kon-Tiki Expedition* ignites worldwide controversy. | | **1950–1953:** Korean War. |
| **1953:** Thor leads an expedition to the Galápagos Islands. | | |

| Historical Milestone | Year | Biographical Milestone |
|---|---|---|

**1955**

**1955–1956:** Thor heads an expedition to Easter Island.

**1957:** Norway's King Olaf V begins his reign.

**Nov. 1963:** President John F. Kennedy is assassinated in Dallas, Texas.

**1969:** First attempt to cross the Atlantic in a reed boat, *Ra,* ends in failure.

**1970**

**1970:** *Ra II* succeeds in crossing the Atlantic, sailing from Morocco to Barbados.

**Aug. 1974:** President Richard Nixon resigns from office.

**1977:** Thor heads the *Tigris* expedition to Africa.

**1980:** The United States boycotts the summer Olympic games in Moscow.

**1982–1984:** Thor leads an expedition to the Maldive Islands.

**1985**

**1989:** Thor begins an excavation of the pyramids at Tucume, Peru.

**1991:** King Olaf V dies.

*Prologue*

# COURAGE

ourage is among the most noble of virtues. Without it, even the simplest task can seem overwhelming. One thousand years ago the Vikings of northern Europe were the most fearless explorers on earth. In narrow wooden boats, with jutting prows and billowing sails, these wild seafarers roamed the oceans, even crossing the Atlantic Ocean to the Canadian coast.

For many, Thor Heyerdahl is the last Viking. Like his ancestors, the sea is in his blood, and so, too, is their

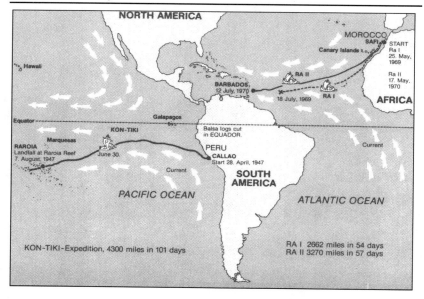

*This map shows Thor Heyerdahl's expeditions.*

fantastic bravery. For decades this Norwegian explorer has pitted himself against nature's might — merciless storms, scorching suns — and risked death from thirst — in order to test himself and his theories. Sometimes the elements have won, but he has never been beaten.

In the same way, Thor has weathered a tidal wave of personal criticism. Ivory-tower scholars, their knowledge of the world gleaned from scientific papers, have launched ferocious attacks on his work. Many find his theories preposterous. Some accuse him of arrogance, of shuffling the evidence to suit his case.

None, though, has questioned Thor's courage.

Thor was born into a changing world. By 1914 science was gaining the upper hand over imagination,

His publications greatly influenced the general public, but he has not convinced scientists.

—José Garanger, writer, 1991

and every corner of the globe had been reached — it seemed the days of explorers were over. But in Thor, the traditional values of discovery and fearlessness found the perfect modern embodiment. He showed that, with an abundance of courage, all things are possible.

**Points to Ponder**

◆ What does the word courage mean to you?

◆ Whom do you know personally who is particularly courageous?

*Chapter 1*

# ISOLATION
# IN A CROWD

om! Mom! Come quick!"
Throbbing with excitement,
the boy stomped impatiently
up the wooden steps that led up to the front door. Inside
the timber-built house, Alison Heyerdahl frowned. What
on earth did her young son want now? Moving quickly
through the neatly furnished rooms, she reached the front

door. As she opened it, bright Norwegian sunshine streamed in. Then she screamed.

Dangling from her son's hand was a live, angry snake.

Thor Heyerdahl beamed triumphantly as he held aloft the thrashing reptile. Even at this early age he was afraid of nothing. Alison gasped as he expertly avoided the venomous reptile's razor-sharp fangs. Thor found the snake in the woods and had carried it more than four miles — first in one outstretched hand, then the other. Now it was to be the prize exhibit in the "zoological museum" that Thor kept in an outbuilding behind his father's brewery.

*Thor thought the reading of fiction was a poor substitute for reality; he wanted to experience life for himself.*

—Arnold Jacoby, a boyhood friend, 1967

Despite her concern, Alison was secretly delighted that the respect and deep love she had for the natural world had been passed on to her only child. Even so, this latest acquisition did make her wonder. Ordinarily, Thor's zoological museum contained butterflies, seashells, hedgehogs, maybe the occasional bat — but a snake!

Thor was born October 6, 1914, and right from his earliest days it was clear that he was very different from the other boys growing up in the little whaling port of

Larvik. While they preferred to hang around the bustling dockside to watch salt-caked ships unload cargoes of oil and blubber, Thor liked to roam the woods, studying its wildlife. Worried that Thor was becoming too academic, his father, also named Thor, tried hard to interest the boy in more "manly" pursuits.

> "Would you like to go hunting today, son?"
>
> "Sorry, Dad, I've got to catalog my collection."
>
> "Not even for some extra pocket money?"
>
> "No, thanks. I'm not interested in shooting animals for sport," replied Thor, busying himself with his specimens, and showing, even at this early age, the firmness of purpose that would dominate his life.

For Thor's father it was another battle lost. Despite owning the local brewery and being a well-respected businessman, he was unable to find happiness at home. His marriage had been a disaster. Alison was simply too strong for him. Strident and self-assured, she dominated her timid husband and was determined that young Thor would grow up sharing her independent spirit.

Alison also encouraged Thor's vivid imagination. When he was eight years old, Thor painted a small picture of a South Sea island, his idea of paradise. Through the long, dark Scandinavian winters he dreamed of traveling to Polynesia in the Pacific Ocean, where the sun shone all the time.

Although not a hunter, as he grew into his teenage years Thor showed he had inherited his ancestors' love of the wild. Norway is a long and narrow country. Its rugged land mass juts up into the Arctic Circle. Although barely larger than New Mexico, Norway has a coastline of more than 12,000 miles due to the hundreds of deep fjords carved out by the Ice Age. It is this coast that has bred the Norwegian's urge to travel.

Thor spent his summer vacations in the mountains above Lillehammer. There, on the edge of the Hoy Fjell, a wild plateau among the craggy peaks, he met Ola Bjorneby, a hermit who had left his wealthy family and civilization to live in a log cabin. Thor greatly admired Ola's irrepressible good humor and from him learned about survival in the wilderness. For the first time, Thor learned how to hunt and fish for his food, how to make do with a stone for a pillow and, most of all, how to overcome hardship.

Before he reached his teens, Thor's parents split up. Because he had never been that close to either parent, Thor took the break in stride. Besides, he had other things on his mind. The Polynesian dream had become an obsession. More than ever he wanted to experience it firsthand. But he needed a partner, someone to travel with him.

He found her at the high school prom.

Liv Torp's classical Scandinavian beauty — masses of blond hair and vivid blue eyes — left

Thor tongue-tied at first. But gradually he overcame his shyness and that evening as they strolled the jetty, he suddenly turned to Liv and blurted out, "What do you think about going back to nature?"

Liv leveled a steady blue gaze at the urgent young man. "It would have to be all the way," she replied coolly.

Thor felt his heart leap. His search was over!

That same year — 1933 — he moved to Oslo to study zoology at the university. While there he met Bjarne Kroepelien, a wealthy wine merchant who owned the world's finest library on Polynesia. This only served to further fuel Thor's imagination. The following year Liv joined Thor at the university and the two planned their future. With the help of a loan from his father, plus a zoological grant, Thor raised enough money to finance their fantasy trip to Polynesia. On Christmas Eve 1936, he and Liv married. The next day they left Norway in search of paradise.

---

### Points to Ponder

◆ What positive influences do you think Thor gained from his parents' unhappy marriage?

◆ How much impact do you think Ola Bjorneby had on the young Thor?

*Chapter 2*

# THE GARDEN
# OF EDEN

Six weeks after boarding a French ocean liner at Marseilles, the honeymooners arrived in Tahiti, on the other side of the world. They were greeted by Chief Teriieroo, the most senior of Tahiti's seventeen chiefs, and a close friend of Bjarne Kroepelien. For several weeks he took the young couple under his wing, teaching them how to live off the

*In 1937, Thor and Liv Heyerdahl spent some of their honeymoon on Fatu Hiva, part of the Marquesas Islands, located in the South Pacific. (Kon-Tiki Museum, Oslo, Norway)*

land, how to distinguish the roots and fruits that were safe to eat from those that were poisonous and how to trap and cook wild pigs. Then they were off again.

The final leg of their marathon journey came with a three-week voyage to the Marquesas Islands, in French Polynesia, aboard a little schooner called the *Tereora*. The master of this ship was a grizzled seafarer named Captain Brander. He sailed the South Seas, trading Western goods for copra, the dried kernel of the coconut.

Late at night, sitting on deck to catch a cooling breeze, the old captain would share his worries about the future of the islands with his young passengers.

"It's crazy," Captain Brander said sadly. "I detest our own civilization. That's why I'm here. Yet I spread it from island to island."

Thor nodded. In his brief time spent on Tahiti, he had already witnessed the corrosive effects of Western civilization and realized its potential harm. He was disturbed by the heavy-handed way the French police and colonial bureaucrats ordered the natives around and tried to make them behave like Frenchmen. For now, though, he had to put all that behind him. He and Liv had reached their destination.

Fatu Hiva was little more than a tiny speck of rock in the Marquesas Islands. But this was the place where Thor and Liv had decided to carry out their great experiment. After bidding them an emotional good-bye, Captain Brander set the couple ashore on the beach.

Standing together on the sand, Thor and Liv watched the *Tereora* sail away across the sparkling blue sea, until it dipped beneath the horizon and vanished.

Only now did they realize the enormity of their venture. Beside them, in two suitcases, were the clothes and effects of two young European travelers, including Liv's wedding gown and a dinner jacket that Thor wore aboard the French liner. What use were they now?

Although very wild, Fatu Hiva was not a deserted island and the new arrivals were soon befriended by Willy Grenet, a local storekeeper. He showed them the best places to live. In the dense forest, beside a dancing stream,

Thor marked out the spot where he would build their house.

For three days Thor hacked at the wild vegetation with his machete, clearing enough space for a hut. The locals, amused by Thor's limited construction skills, soon bartered their house-building services for the contents of the suitcases. Within days the Heyerdahls were the proud owners of a sturdy hut made from plaited bamboo and topped with a woven coconut-leaf roof.

*He's fantastic . . . a great organizer . . . to me he's much more a friend than a scientist.*

—*Øystein Koch Johansen, Thor's colleague and later director of the Kon-Tiki Museum, 1994*

At first Fatu Hiva turned out to be the "Garden of Eden" that Thor and Liv had hoped for. They bathed in crystal-clear pools, ate fruit picked off the vine and became attuned to the island's slow pace. True, life was hard, but it was endlessly fascinating and it did allow Thor time to flex his imagination. In particular, he was curious as to how these islands had been populated.

One day he was taken to see some rock carvings. These showed figures six feet high and sailing boats with steep-angled bows. If these were the original settlers, as the natives claimed, Thor wondered where they had come from. What were their origins?

Soon, though, all thoughts of ancient history had to be cast aside — paradise had turned ugly.

It began with a mystery illness that swept the island, killing off the natives. Thor and Liv were relatively unaffected, beyond a mild flu, but their friends were dying. Then came torrential rains, turning everything into a sea of mud. Even worse was the sudden plague of mosquitoes. This time there was no escape. Liv was covered in boils, Thor in sores. The nearest medical help was on the island of Hivaoa, sixty miles away. In desperation, and with a few natives to help them, the couple set sail in an abandoned wooden lifeboat they had found.

The voyage was terrifying. Huge seas threatened to swamp them with every wave. Hour after hour they bailed water until, exhausted, they reached Hivaoa. It had been a horrific ordeal that took great courage and left Thor with a lifetime suspicion of wooden boats.

Slowly their health recovered. One day their nurse took them to a remote part of the island to meet a fellow Norwegian, Henry Lie. He showed them huge, red, stone statues with bulging eyes and grinning mouths weighing many tons. Again Thor was puzzled. Who had built them?

In a book he found pictures of similar statues in South America. He read how the locals told the Spanish conquistadors that they had been made, not by their ancestors, but by fair-skinned people who had later set out on balsa-wood rafts across the Pacific, toward the setting sun. Thor's heart pounded. This tied in with native lore on Hivaoa that spoke of light-skinned settlers with reddish hair, who were already present when the Polynesians arrived.

With these questions to ponder, he and Liv returned to Fatu Hiva, only to find that in just a few weeks the jungle had reclaimed their home. For a while they lived with the island's last surviving cannibal. He told them about Tiki, the god-king, who had led his ancestors from across the ocean to these islands from the east. Years later Thor would learn that the full name of this god-king was Con-Tici, or Kon-Tiki, known more simply as Tiki.

Thor began to study the island vegetation. Much of it — the papaya, the small pineapple and the sweet potato — originated in South America. How had these plants traveled thousands of miles to this place? At times his preoccupation became hypnotic.

> "I sat and marveled at this sea which never stopped proclaiming that it came this way, rolling in from the east, from the east, from the east . . . ."

However, none of Thor's excitement could overcome the fact that he and Liv had tired of their great experiment. Worn out and reduced to living in a cave like Stone Age people, the couple decided it was time to leave.

In March 1938 they returned to Norway. Thor wrote about their adventures in *In Search of Paradise*. In his eyes the trip had been a great success. He might not have found paradise, but he had found his vocation: He would be an explorer.

## Points to Ponder

◆ What would you miss most, if, like Thor and Liv, you traveled halfway around the world to live on a tropical island?

◆ Was Captain Brander right to be so pessimistic about the future of the islands?

◆ Thor believed that the fruit plants on Fatu Hiva could have been brought only by the first settlers. Can you think of any other way in which those fruit seeds might have been carried to the islands?

*Chapter 3*

# AGAINST THE WIND

The questions that had baffled Thor on Fatu Hiva now became an obsession with him. Where had those first settlers come from? All the textbooks stated that Polynesia had been settled from Asia. This made no sense to Thor. There are two main currents in the Pacific Ocean. In the north, the Urdarneta Route runs from west to east. South of the equator, the main Pacific current is the Mendana Route, which runs in the opposite direction, from east to west.

This suggested to Thor that early Asiatic explorers were far more likely to have first set sail for North America across the northern Pacific, then traveled south, through present-day Central America to countries like Peru. Only then did they sail due east to Polynesia.

When he learned that in western Canada there were rock carvings remarkably similar to those on Fatu Hiva, he and Liv, with their recently born son, Thor Jr., packed their bags and moved to British Columbia.

Then, in April 1940, came tragedy — Norway was invaded by the rampaging German army. Thor, determined to fight for his homeland, signed on with a special unit known as Little Norway. Through no fault of their own, the volunteers languished in Canada for much of the war, cooling their heels while Allied commanders worked out how best to employ them.

Eventually, Thor received orders to return to occupied Europe. After making sure that Liv and the baby were safe with friends in New York, he set off with a convoy that landed in Murmansk in the Soviet Union. From there it was a long march across the frozen wastes until he reached Norway.

It was the greatest homecoming of his life. "Never since has any arrival in Norway filled me with such profuse joy," he later said. Thor spent the remainder of the war behind enemy lines, serving with a parachute regiment, until 1945, when Germany surrendered.

*After several unsuccessful attempts to promote his idea of sailing across the Pacific on a balsa-wood raft, Thor finally found some enthusiastic supporters at the Explorer's Club in New York. From left to right: Chief of Clannfhearghuls, Herman Watzinger, Thor, and Greenland explorer Peter Freuchen discuss plans for the ocean voyage. (Kon-Tiki Museum, Oslo, Norway)*

Peacetime brought its own problems. Liv, left alone to bring up two young sons, urged Thor to devote more time to being a father and husband. Even as she spoke Liv realized that the years of separation had driven a wedge between them. Thor had no intention of settling down.

He returned to New York, where he visited the famous Explorer's Club. Its president, Dr. Herbert Spinden, listened patiently to Thor's theory of migration before shaking his head.

*You can't treat ethnographic problems as a sort of detective mystery . . . the task of science is investigation pure and simple, not to prove this or that.*

—Dr. Herbert Spinden, 1946

"None of the peoples of South America got over to the islands in the Pacific," Spinden said. "Do you know why? The answer's simple enough. They couldn't get there. They had no boats."

"They had rafts," Thor protested, "balsa-wood rafts."

Spinden smiled benignly. "Would you like to try a trip from Peru to the Pacific Islands on a balsa-wood raft?"

Thor had no answer to that. The old man patted him kindly on the shoulder and showed him out. It was the same everywhere — Washington, Boston, New York — everyone thought Thor was a crank obsessed by a crackpot idea. Doors slammed shut in his face. Depressed and down to his last few dollars, Thor booked into the Sailors' Home in New York.

There, he met a Norwegian, Herman Watzinger. An engineer by training, Watzinger listened to Thor with mounting enthusiasm and agreed to join him in attempting the impossible — to build a balsa-wood raft and sail it thousands of miles across the Pacific.

It sounded like madness, but when renowned Greenland traveler Peter Freuchen threw his weight behind the scheme, offers of financial backing began to trickle in. Soon there was enough to begin serious planning.

Thor gave careful thought to the other crew members. Two obvious candidates were Knut Haugland and Torstein Raaby, two wartime friends from the Norwegian resistance and both radio specialists. Another was boyhood friend Erik Hesselberg, an expert navigator. Each received a letter from Thor that read:

> Am going to cross the Pacific on a wooden raft to support a theory that the South Sea Islands were peopled from Peru. Will you come?

All three jumped at the chance.

Thor wanted six people on board the raft in order to carry out watches of four hours each. He was one crew member short. However, he was in no hurry. Instinct told him that in time the right man would appear. (He had decided against taking any women on the voyage because of the cramped quarters and fear of adverse publicity.)

Meanwhile, Thor and Herman traveled to Peru to search out a suitable place in which to build their raft. Once again Thor's fantastic powers of persuasion came through. He managed to gain an audience with the president of Peru, a man rarely seen in public.

After considering what Thor had to say, the president said, "If it is possible that the Pacific Islands were first discovered from Peru, then Peru has an interest in this expedition." Extending a hand for Thor to shake, he said, "Let us be partners." He then granted permission to use the naval docks at Callao.

It was around this time that a tall, bearded man in tropical gear presented himself at Thor's hotel room.

"Bengt Danielsson," the stranger said by way of introduction. "I've just heard about the raft plans."

Thor had heard of Danielsson, an eminent ethnologist from Sweden. He waited for the expected outburst of criticism. It never came.

"I've come to ask if I may come with you on the raft," said the Swede. "I'm interested in the migration theory."

Thor grinned his delight. The crew was complete. Now it was time to build the raft.

---

### Points to Ponder

◆ If someone asked you to suddenly undertake a hazardous trip halfway around the world, what would be your reaction?

◆ Can you imagine what went through Liv's mind as she watched her husband pursue his dream?

## Chapter 4

# BUILDING
# A DREAM

On one point Thor was adamant — no modern materials such as nails or wire would be used in the raft's construction. Everything had to be natural. In the early sixteenth century, the conquering Spaniards had been amazed at the quality of the balsa-wood rafts built by the native South American tribes, and had described these craft in great detail. Close study of these designs convinced Thor of their timeless common sense.

*The* Kon-Tiki *was built in Peru out of nine large balsa logs. The raft was held together by hemp ropes, with no nails or metal used in any manner.*

Finding suitable balsa logs proved a real problem. Thor wanted newly felled trees because old logs would absorb water at too fast a rate, and thus run the risk of sinking. After scouring Peru, he eventually found the ideal trees in nearby Ecuador. A dozen logs, each weighing about a ton, were dragged to the river Palenque, first by horse, then by tractor. These were lashed together to form two temporary rafts, which were then carried along by the river's current to the port of Guayaquil, on the coast of Ecuador. From there the logs were shipped by steamer to Callao, eight hundred miles to the south.

Nine of the thickest logs were laid side by side to form the basis of the raft. Each was allowed to assume its natural floating position before being lashed to the next. The longest log — forty-five feet in length — was laid in the middle of the raft and projected out a long way at both ends.

The four logs on either side were cut progressively shorter, so that the outer log was about thirty feet long. Across this framework, other, smaller logs were laid, then topped with a deck made from split bamboo. More than 300 ropes were used to lash the entire structure together.

Toward the rear of the deck was a small, open cabin, fashioned from plaited bamboo reeds and banana leaves. In front of the cabin were two huge masts, placed side by side. The masts were cut from iron-hard mangrove wood and were strong enough to hold the big, rectangular square sail.

Piece by piece, among the gray submarines and warships that filled the Callao dockyard, Thor's dream began to take shape. Curious onlookers chuckled as the young Scandinavians toiled on their odd-looking craft.

*. . . this modern-day Ulysses.*

—National Geographic Magazine
*describing Thor Heyerdahl, 1997*

Old sea dogs, too, doubted Thor's sanity. Many even laughed. Not one thought the craft had any chance of completing its voyage. One Peruvian navy admiral who inspected the craft told the crew that, in his opinion, they were as good as dead already!

Unaffected by the jokes and scoffing, the crew members went about their work with increasing urgency. Under the bamboo deck they stowed enough provisions to last them for four months. Although Thor estimated the trip would take one hundred days, he had food for an additional three weeks. Each man was rationed to half a gallon of water a day. There was no room to take more. At the last minute fresh fruit, vegetables, and coconuts were stowed on deck in large wicker baskets.

Then came the great day.

On April 28, 1947, towed by a powerful tug, the tiny raft nudged out of Callao Harbor and into the Pacific, the world's largest ocean. Ahead lay a 4,000-mile trip into the unknown.

The next day, as the tug sailed from view back toward the coast, Raaby joked, "Now we'll have to start the engine, boys," a reference to the wind that had suddenly blown up.

Thor had no doubts that the trade winds would be his ally, just as they had helped the Peruvian sun god, who, legend said, had migrated to the west countless generations earlier. As a mark of respect to this mythical sun god, Thor named his little balsa-wood raft *Kon-Tiki*.

## Points to Ponder

◆ What other attributes besides courage do you think Thor exhibited in getting his dream off the ground?

◆ What would be your reaction if someone forecast that you were sailing to your death?

*Chapter 5*

# THE JOURNEY
# OF A LIFETIME

Slowly the big, orange sail filled as *Kon-Tiki* caught the Humboldt Current, which sweeps up from the Antarctic to Peru and then swings west across the Pacific Ocean just south of the equator. Within hours the wisdom of the raft's construction was made crystal clear to all on board. Whenever a large wave crashed over the side, the water ran through the gaps between the logs. The more leaks the better. Had *Kon-Tiki* been a conventional boat, they would have been bailing nonstop.

At three o'clock on the morning of April 30, they spotted a ship's light to the north. They used their flashlight to signal but the ship never responded.

They would not see another ship for three months.

Soon the men fell into a routine, two hours at the steering oar during the day, another two hours at night. The rest of the time was spent performing other tasks or else reading. At night Hesselberg's folksinging talents were put to good use, his voice and guitar echoing eerily across the silent, black water.

Always the ocean was the master. Thor knew that. His greatest fear was that the balsa-wood raft would become waterlogged and simply sink. Once, unobserved, Thor broke off a piece of wood, threw it overboard and watched it vanish in seconds. Later, he saw other crew members do the same. Nothing was said; nothing needed to be said. Everyone knew the risks.

There was good news on one front, though. The ropes, far from rubbing together and snapping like all the experts forecasted, actually wore grooves in the soft balsa wood and thus became protected.

Steadily, *Kon-Tiki* sailed westward, carried along by the current and the trade winds.

With each passing day the crew members felt themselves withdraw from the cares of civilization. Their beards and unkempt hair gave them the look of ancient Vikings. But not even the great Viking navigators had journeyed this far.

The *Kon-Tiki* heads toward Polynesia. (Kon-Tiki Museum, Oslo, Norway)

Out here, in the middle of the Pacific Ocean, all that mattered were the elements. Which way was the wind blowing? How strong? What were the clouds doing? Was that a storm over there? Above all, it was a time for self-exploration.

*Thor builds his pyramids upside down.*

—Bengt Danielsson,
*implying that Thor tended to reach a conclusion, then
searched for the evidence to support it, 1950*

Danger was ever present. Once, when Haugland was washing some clothes, a whale shark, the largest fish in the world, capable of reaching fifty feet in length and weighing fifteen tons, suddenly reared out of the water in front of him. His cry of alarm brought everyone running.

They watched in silent horror as the monster circled the raft. The whale shark was so huge that his head would be on one side of the raft while his huge tail lashed dangerously on the other. No one dared breathe. A single swish of the animal's tail would smash *Kon-Tiki* to splinters. Finally, Hesselberg could stand it no more. Grabbing a harpoon, he flung it at the inquisitive creature with all his might.

It struck home!

At once the enraged giant dived for the depths, peeling off rope at a manic rate. The thick line, strong enough to hold the raft, snapped like a piece of twine. Suddenly, two hundred yards away, a broken-off harpoon shaft rose to the surface. Then the ocean fell silent.

Everyone braced himself. Surely this monster, maddened by the attack, would return seeking revenge. But the water remained quiet. The brush with death was over, at least for now.

Nobody had enjoyed wounding the shark, but this was all about survival. The creature could have easily killed them.

Then it was back to the routine. Thor led by example, either steering the boat with the single oar that served as a rudder or else navigating. All of the on-board duties were delegated fairly. Haugland and Raaby, the radio experts, each took turns broadcasting regular weather reports to short-wave radio enthusiasts for onward transmission to the Meteorological Institute in Washington, D.C. Hesselberg, the main navigator, made sure that the raft remained on its proper course. Cooking chores were shared.

Any anxieties the crew may have had about running short of food and water were soon allayed by the ocean's bounty and the regular heavy showers that filled their water containers. Often it was unnecessary to throw lines and hooks, as bonitos (a type of fish) and flying fish propelled themselves on deck. On one memorable occasion, a fish literally flew into the frying pan!

Overall the weather was good. But no ocean slumbers forever, and one day a massive storm blew up. In just minutes the previously tranquil waters were whipped to a fearsome frenzy, hurling waves twenty-five feet high at the tiny raft. The crew's anxious expressions soon gave way to smiles of relief as *Kon-Tiki* bobbed along like a cork, up one wave and down the next, seemingly unsinkable. Every crashing breaker was a testament to Thor's belief that this was how the first explorers had crossed the Pacific, aboard balsa-wood rafts just like this one.

Even if *Kon-Tiki* was immune to the worst that the Pacific could throw at it, it was soon clear that the crew was not. During another storm, disaster almost struck. Watzinger was measuring the storm's wind speed when a sudden gust swept Raaby's sleeping bag overboard.

Instinctively Watzinger reached to grab it, only to tumble in himself. Although a strong swimmer, his attempts to stay level with the raft were foiled by the huge waves that kept inching him farther away.

"Man overboard!"

As Thor fought to free the small rescue dinghy, Haugland and Hesselberg threw out a life belt, only to see it hurled back by the mocking wind. Far off in the water, Watzinger's cries for help and his strength were both fading fast.

Just when all seemed lost, Haugland dived into the water clutching the life belt. Bravely he struck out toward his stricken friend. At times both men disappeared beneath the surging waves. First one could be seen, then the other. Then they surfaced together. By a miracle, both managed to grab hold of the life belt while the remaining crew members worked fervently to haul them in. Eventually, more dead than alive, the two men were dragged to safety.

It had been the closest of close calls.

## Points to Ponder

◆ Were the crew members justified in throwing the harpoon at the whale shark?

◆ Do you think that bravery is contagious, or is it simply that anyone who attempted such a trip would automatically have to be brave?

*Chapter 6*

# LANDFALL!

he night of July 30 was hot and sticky. Sleep was almost impossible for the men inside the cabin. Cries of lone sea-birds could be heard occasionally. Then suddenly the cries began to merge into one deafening roar as hundreds of birds wheeled overhead in the night sky. Instantly the men were awake. This could only mean one thing — land!

Squinting through the pale dawn light, their eyes scanned every inch of the ocean.

"There! Over there!" someone cried.

Far off on the horizon a tiny island glinted in the light of the rising sun. A quick inspection of their charts revealed that they must have drifted north during the night. Now it was too late. The current was sweeping them ever westward. They had missed their first chance to make landfall, but surely others would come soon.

With this exciting prospect came a serious problem, one that Thor had not even considered — he had no idea how to stop *Kon-Tiki!*

Nor did anyone else onboard. Now, this oversight threatened disaster. The coral atoll islands of eastern Polynesia are surrounded by jagged reefs that can tear a boat to shreds. Without any engine, a raft like *Kon-Tiki* was entirely at the mercy of the wind and sea. Thor believed that the earliest settlers from South America overcame this problem because they used vast flotillas of rafts. Even if most were destroyed, some would find a way through the reef to safety.

*Kon-Tiki* had no such backup.

A genuine fear gripped everyone onboard. All they could do was hope.

Just days later they spotted the island of Angatau, part of the Tuamotu Archipelago. The sun was low in the sky as Thor fought to steer a path through the protective coral barrier. Beyond, he could see inquisitive natives on the beach. Then a canoe was launched. He watched in admiration as two men expertly navigated a gap in the reef. They waved. Thor waved back. Other canoes joined them. One came alongside the raft and took Haugland aboard. But he was the only crew member to actually land on Angatau. *Kon-Tiki* had to remain outside the reef, waiting for another chance to make landfall.

*He is an explorer who embodies just that "spirit of quest"which so distinguished the heroes of the past.*

—Tim Heald, noted writer, 1980

It came three days later on August 7. And it proved to be every bit as terrifying as Thor had feared. The notorious Takume and Raroia Reefs stretch for almost fifty miles along the Tuamotu Archipelago, and every inch is packed with danger. With contemptuous ease the ocean picked up *Kon-Tiki* and began hurling her toward the reef.

Every man grabbed his life belt. This was the critical moment, the time when victory — and perhaps much more — could be snatched from their grasp. They braced themselves for the battle to come. A sudden, massive wave swept over them. Hands clutched for ropes, logs, masts, anything to hang on to.

"Look out!" yelled Thor as another wave, even bigger than the first, bore down on them.

"Hold on! Hold on!"

For an instant the entire world was swallowed up by seething green water. Men were tossed around like puppets as the thunderous wave flung them forward. With a huge crash, *Kon-Tiki* smashed into the reef. Miraculously, everyone survived. Ahead, some six or seven hundred yards across a shallow lagoon, lay a tropical island. All the men were able to wade the last few triumphant yards of their journey to an island fringed with palm trees and snowy-white beaches.

Thor reached the shoreline, almost delirious with delight, took off his shoes and let the warm, dry sand run through his toes. Danielsson was more laconic. "Purgatory was a bit damp," he remarked, "but heaven more or less as I'd imagined it."

They all laughed, then someone pointed out across the lagoon. Stranded on the reef, *Kon-Tiki* was taking a terrible pounding. Huge breakers crushed the cabin and everything else on deck, but the nine huge balsa logs, the ones that the experts had said would not last two weeks, were still intact. The heroic little raft had done everything that Thor had asked of her and more. He and his companions had traveled 4,300 miles in 101 days.

One of the great voyages in history was over.

## Points to Ponder

◆ What kind of feelings do you think the crew members experienced as they made landfall?

◆ If you were at sea for three months, what would you do first after you made landfall?

## Chapter 7

# UNDER ATTACK

For Thor it was a dream come true. By putting his own life on the line, he had proved that South American natives could have populated Polynesia. Coming hard on the heels of World War II, with all the misery and deaths it had caused, the *Kon-Tiki*'s inspiring voyage made Thor a global hero. It was the first great adventure of the postwar era, and for millions in Europe particularly, faced with the day-to-day tedium of food rationing and deprivation, this South Seas adventure was the stuff of dreams. Thor himself was amazed by all the interest, especially when a film of the venture, recorded on a

*Members of the* Kon-Tiki *expedition became international heroes. At the White House, Thor gave President Harry S. Truman the American flag, carried on board the Kon-Tiki. From left to right: (slightly hidden) Knut Haugland, Thor, Herman Watzinger, President Truman, Mr. Lykke (counselor to the Norwegian Embassy), Erik Hesselberg and Torstein Raaby. (Kon-Tiki Museum, Oslo, Norway)*

primitive camera, won an Oscar for the year's best documentary.

*A nice adventure, but you don't expect anybody to call that a scientific expedition. Now, do you?*

—Sir Peter Buck, an authority on Polynesia, 1950

Thor's account of the voyage, *The Kon-Tiki Expedition*, published in 1950, went on to sell more than 20 million copies and was translated into every major language. But not everyone was pleased. Far from it. The academic world turned viciously on this interloper.

Sir Peter Buck, a leading authority on Polynesia, counting Pacific Islanders among his own ancestors, summed up the general attitude.

"Those Norwegians want us to believe their pre-Inca Peruvians were doing a bit of coastal fishing and got picked up by the Humboldt Current and eventually wound up alive and safe somewhere to father the Polynesian race. Well, no fisherman I ever saw had women aboard. And by their own theory the landings were made on uninhabited islands — so who exactly was going to mother our Polynesian peoples?"

Although a gross oversimplification of his ideas, this reaction was an early indicator to Thor of the strange duality of his success. The ordinary person worshiped him as a hero, but those few scientists who did condescend to study the *Kon-Tiki* expedition were scathing in their attacks. In Finland, one professor virtually accused Thor of faking the whole enterprise, while another academic from Denmark announced it would be better if the subject were "killed by silence."

It was now that Thor had to be at his toughest. Taming the tempestuous ocean had been nothing compared to this.

Steely in his self-resolve, Thor buried himself in another book, a huge volume entitled *American Indians in the Pacific,* in which he advanced his theory of diffusionism.

Diffusionism argues that close similarities between two or more cultures, whether they take the form of religious worship, pottery or burial customs, can be taken as evidence of physical contact. The problem has always been in explaining how this contact had been established.

Thor felt he had already proved one connection. But he was always on the lookout for others. Already he was casting his eye around the globe, wondering where the next challenge lay.

His gaze settled on the Galápagos Islands. Situated in the Pacific, approximately six hundred miles west of Ecuador, the Galápagos are curious and strange. Bizarre animals are found here that occur nowhere else in the world, and this is where the nineteenth-century naturalist Charles Darwin formulated his revolutionary theories of

# NOBODY'S PERFECT

Among the many criticisms leveled at Thor were accusations that he was ruthless in his pursuit of publicity. His flair for self-promotion was evident in everything he did. But at least one person suspected that he was not above manipulating even the most personal moments for his own ends.

Liv was at Washington Airport when Thor returned in triumph after the *Kon-Tiki* expedition. As she rushed out across the tarmac to greet and kiss him, a photographer dashed forward to record the moment on film. Convinced, based on previous experience, that Thor had stage-managed the whole incident for publicity purposes, Liv angrily pushed her husband away.

Thor found the humiliation unforgivable. As for Liv, all the bitterness of separation now bubbled over inside her. Almost single-handedly she had raised two sons. Also, she had abandoned her own promising academic career in order that Thor might realize his dreams. Now she felt used and betrayed.

Even before this incident, cracks had been appearing in their marriage. Both realized it was time for a new beginning. Shortly afterward, they divorced.

*Easter Island in 1955. (Kon-Tiki Museum, Oslo, Norway)*

natural selection in the animal kingdom. Thor, however, was more interested in human evolution.

Thor had been drawn by rumors of statues, allegedly carved by settlers hundreds of years previously. When he landed in 1953, Thor didn't find any statues, but he did find fragments of ceramic pottery identical to those found in Ecuador and Peru — further ammunition to defend his belief that the ancient South Americans had the navigational skills to master the world's largest ocean.

By studying ancient drawings, Thor also learned how the South American explorers had maneuvered their balsa rafts. It was all done through a series of movable centerboards. That, combined with skillful manipulation of the sail, made it possible for a balsa-wood raft to tack against the wind.

While his Galápagos studies provided only scanty evidence to support his theories, Thor refused to be downcast. Already he was planning his next great adventure.

Easter Island is one of the most remote spots on earth. The island had first been discovered by Europeans on Easter Sunday 1722, when the Dutch navigator Jacob Roggeveen landed. He was puzzled by two things. First, the natives differed widely in their skin coloring — some were quite light, while others were dark — and second, he was baffled by their religious rituals. Along the cliffs they had erected more than four hundred enormous stone statues, which they worshiped as the sun rose from the sea in the east.

Like all subsequent explorers, Roggeveen was puzzled by how such massive statues had been erected, for there seemed to be no solid wood or strong rope available.

When Thor arrived in October 1955, he was determined to unravel the mystery. He also wanted to learn more about the so-called Long Ears, the light-skinned settlers from the east who had built these statues. Everywhere he traveled, it seemed, he heard stories of these fabled explorers.

A local mayor, Pedro Atan, claimed to be a direct descendant of these Long Ears and he provided Thor with a vivid demonstration of how his ancestors had first carved the statues, then raised them using mounds of stones, poles and ropes. Atan explained the strange absence of trees on the island, noting that they had all been cut down to provide the wooden levers used to raise the statues.

*A young man who... proves that a long list of distinguished professors have been wrong, cannot count on any mercy. No one likes to lose face.*

—Professor Kristian Gleditsch,
president of the Norwegian Geographical Society,
1952

As in the past, Thor kept a meticulous diary of his time on Easter Island, and again turned his experiences into a best-selling book, *Aku-Aku: The Secret of Easter Island*. Equally predictable was the reaction of the scientists — they attacked his theories and beliefs.

## Points to Ponder

- ◆ Fame has changed many people. What do you consider to be the main drawbacks to being famous?

- ◆ Do you feel Liv was justified in suspecting that Thor had exploited her?

- ◆ Why do you think Thor has provoked such savage criticism?

*Chapter 8*

# THE PAPER BOATS

*T*hor refused to abandon his theory of
diffusionism. Every instinct told him that
the world had been settled by vast
oceanic voyages, not land-based migrations, as was
generally believed. One of his favorite sayings is, "The
sail came before the saddle," and in the late 1960s he
became intrigued by the possibility that ancient Egyptian
mariners had sailed far beyond the Mediterranean —
perhaps even across the Atlantic Ocean! Were these the
mysterious "Long Ears"?

Traditional historians scoffed. How could the Egyptians have possibly tackled the Atlantic? In papyrus reed boats? (Papyrus, used to make paper in ancient Egypt, was also used to build boats.) Even the president of the Egyptian Papyrus Institute was skeptical.

"Papyrus sinks after two week," he sniffed, on hearing of Thor's hypothesis.

Thor wasn't so certain. All around the world, in Mexico and in Lake Titicaca in Bolivia, as well as in Egypt, he'd seen similarly designed reed boats at work. Papyrus reeds were tough. And there was something else. Throughout Polynesia the natives called the sun god Ra. In Egypt they used the same name. Just a coincidence? Or was it possible that the Egyptians were, indeed, far superior seafarers than was generally believed?

There was only way to find out.

In the shadow of the Egyptian pyramids, Thor's latest dream took shape — a boat made from some 280,000 reeds, each approximately ten feet long, all brought from Lake Trana in the Ethiopian highlands. As always, he stuck closely to the original drawings.

The drawings showed a rope connecting the top of the curved prow with the stern of the ship. Experts insisted that the rope's purpose was largely cosmetic, just to keep the prow in place. Thor felt there was some other reason, but grudgingly heeded the experts' advice that the rope was superfluous.

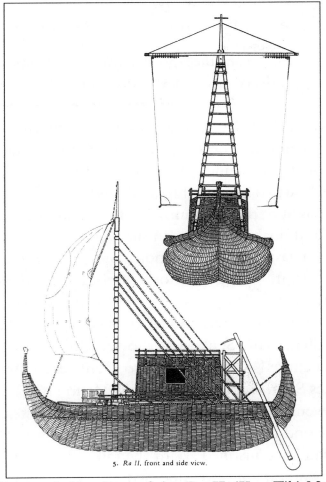

5. *Ra II*, front and side view.

The front and side views of the *Ra II*. (Kon-Tiki Museum, Oslo, Norway)

He was also told no cedarwood could be found for the two oars that would steer the boat. Egyptian timber merchants confidently assured him that local iroko wood would be just as strong. Again, with considerable reluctance, he accepted their advice.

# I name you Ra in honor of the sun-god.

*—Aicha Amara, the representative of the Moroccan
king, at the launching of the papyrus reed boat, 1969*

Eventually the boat was finished, transported to the port of Safi in Morocco, christened with the traditional goat's milk and launched. As it slid down the slipway, Thor's heart was in his throat. Would his "paper boat" sink straight to the bottom? *Ra* hit the water with a loud splash and floated proudly on the waves.

After last-minute alterations and provisioning, the second great voyage of Thor's life began from Safi on May 25, 1969. Thor was fifty-four years old. This time he chose a truly international crew: Abdullah Djibrine from Chad, Yuri Senkevich (Soviet Union), Norman Baker (United States), Santiago Genovese (Mexico), Georges Sourial (Egypt) and Carlo Mauri (Italy).

Seven hours into the voyage, disaster struck. The iroko-wood steering mechanism snapped. Thor's worst fears had been justified. With the sail flapping uselessly, the expedition appeared doomed. Then, suddenly, as if she had a life of her own, *Ra* wheeled about in the current and began sailing westward.

*Ra*'s steady progress across the Atlantic delighted Thor. But there were drawbacks. The pollution, even this far out at sea, was appalling. Plastic bottles and other pieces of trash bobbed on the waves, which themselves were often slicked with a skim of oil.

"It became clear to all of us," he wrote, "that mankind really was in the process of polluting its most vital wellspring, our planet's indispensable filtration plant, the ocean."

In time this would become a central theme of Thor's life, but for now he had other, more urgent problems.

The weather was worsening fast. The relentless Atlantic storms began to take their toll on the little boat. Ominously, the stern began to sink lower and lower in the water, acting as an anchor almost. Thor pounded his fists on the reeds in frustration. Of course! It was all so obvious now! That rope from the prow was no mere decoration but a vital strengthening link, in place to support the weakest part of the boat, its rear, which had now become dangerously unstable.

A huge storm did the rest. Over several days *Ra* increasingly listed starboard. Finally, with more than half their intended journey completed, they had to radio for help. Thor summoned everyone to a meeting. All were for going on. But with sharks circling the boat, Thor decided that the risks were too great and he gave the order to abandon ship. The papyrus boat sailed 2,700 miles in fifty-six days. They were just one week short of landfall in Barbados.

Thor immediately set about organizing a second attempt. At forty feet, *Ra II* was much shorter than her predecessor, and much more rigid in her construction, too. And this time there was the all-important rope from prow to stern.

On May 17, 1970, *Ra II* set sail from Safi with the same crew as before, except that Djibrine dropped out to be replaced by a Berber, Madani Ait Ouhanni. Also onboard was a Japanese film cameraman, Kei Ohara.

The crew noticed an immediate difference in the way she rode through the water. After ditching some unnecessary equipment to increase buoyancy, they learned how to handle the craft and made excellent time. It soon became clear that this was a far more seaworthy vessel. Despite being battered by storms even worse than those encountered on the first voyage, after fifty-seven days at sea, *Ra II* sailed into Bridgetown Harbor, in Barbados, accompanied by a flotilla of fifty boats. They had covered 3,270 miles. Once again Thor had been proved right: Ancient peoples could have crossed vast oceans — even in a "paper boat."

---

## Points to Ponder

◆ Besides courage, Thor's perseverance is also impressive. What effect do you think it had on these two expeditions?

◆ What do you think motivated the hostilities of scholars toward Thor?

*Chapter 9*

# THE FINAL
# VOYAGE

𝓘n 1977 Thor began construction of yet another reed boat. Under his command, and flying the United Nations' flag, the *Tigris* set sail from Iraq, traveling down the Persian Gulf, across the Arabian Sea and toward the Red Sea. The goal was to establish the possibility that the ancient Sumerians might have used similar means to spread their culture through Southwest Asia and the Arabian Peninsula.

Thor proved his point. In four months *Tigris* traveled 4,000 miles and again demonstrated the validity of Thor's diffusionist views. But as it answered questions about the ancient world, it raised new ones about the modern world. The trip took them through sea-lanes crowded with huge oil tankers, and everywhere the ocean was discolored and dirty.

In protest at what they found, the crew decided on a grand gesture. On March 29, 1978, after sending a telegram to Secretary-General Kurt Waldheim of the United Nations protesting the pollution, they burnt *Tigris* at Djibouti. This had symbolic resonance for Thor. Centuries earlier, his ancestors, the Vikings, had also torched their boats, most often in funeral ceremonies. Perhaps it was his way of telling the world that something had died.

I don't know what is his driving force. It's very strange that a man eighty years old continues to see forwards and forwards and forwards.

—Øystein Koch Johansen,
director of the Kon-Tiki Museum, 1994

Thor shows no signs of slowing down. In 1982 he led an archaeological expedition to the Maldives in the

*While sailing aboard the* Tigris, *Thor and his crew became disturbed and angered by the extensive pollution they found far out in the open sea. In protest, they set the* Tigris *afire at Djibouti on March 29, 1978. (Kon-Tiki Museum, Oslo, Norway)*

Indian Ocean to study statues that bore baffling similarities to those found on Easter Island. A return visit to Easter Island two years later confirmed the resemblances. Another major expedition got under way in 1989, when Thor began excavating the huge pyramid complex at Tucume, Peru. More than nine centuries old, Tucume's most exciting revelation has been a frieze depicting reed boats, just like those Thor found in Egypt.

Thor is always seeking support for diffusionism — the single fact that will convince even the harshest skeptic. His own attitude is clear:

"We have been blinded too long by the European attitude that everything began with us. In reality, many great civilizations terminated with our arrival. . . . Personally, I don't believe that civilization simply sprang into existence 5,000 years ago."

Thor's fame has transcended the usual boundaries of exploration. Nowadays, he is truly a universal figure. In February 1994 his voice welcomed the world to the Winter Olympic Games in Lillehammer, Norway. And on April 10, 1997, Thor showed he had lost none of his pioneering spirit when he gave a lecture over the Internet. Much of this lecture was concerned with ecology and the problems facing the planet, which he believes can be solved only by global cooperation.

And, of course, Thor continues to ruffle feathers. In 1995 he caused a storm of outrage with his claim that Christopher Columbus had reached America, not in 1492, but a quarter of a century earlier! Archive material discovered in Denmark and Portugal, Thor said, strongly suggested that Columbus was a sixteen-year-old chartsman on an expedition that reached the Davis Straits, between Greenland and Canada, in 1467. He only retraced the route in 1492.

"The history books will have to be rewritten," said Thor. "Posterity has vastly underestimated Columbus. Many have thought it was just chance that he discovered the Americas in 1492."

Predictably, the reaction was volcanic. "This is palpable rubbish and at variance with every verifiable fact," barked one historian. Thor, unconcerned, merely carried on with his work. There is still so much to do.

As a young lad Thor kept an angry snake at arm's length to avoid its venomous bite. Similarly, traditional scholars snap at him from a distance, irked by the knowledge that, no matter how many times they have tried to kill off Thor's ideas and theories, not once have they been able to categorically prove him wrong.

---

## Points to Ponder

◆ How successful has Thor been in proving his theory of diffusionism?

◆ Do you feel that governments do enough to protect the environment?

◆ In your opinion, how big a part has courage played in Thor's life?

## Epilogue

❀

# SUMMING UP A LIFE

y overcoming some of the toughest challenges that this earth can offer, Thor Heyerdahl achieved heroic status. When he and his companions set sail aboard *Kon-Tiki*, the potential for tragedy was all around. A sudden storm, an error of judgment, and these intrepid explorers might have vanished forever. Instead, under Thor's brave leadership, they sailed into the history books. That kind of inspirational courage is a rare and special thing.

When Thor began, pessimists declared that the golden age of exploration was over. Time and time again he proved them wrong. He sailed the oceans of the world, excavated ancient archaeological sites, campaigned against

*Thor in 1988. (Kon-Tiki Museum, Oslo, Norway)*

the dangers of pollution, wrote at length on all of his exploits, and offered plausible solutions to some of history's greatest riddles.

Born in obscurity, he convinced the world to pay heed to his unfashionable opinions by the daring of his actions. His deeds have brought him close friendships with many of the world's most powerful figures. The honors and decorations they have showered on him are a recognition of the great difference he has made and continues to make.

"I never feel homesick," Thor once said, "because I have nowhere to call home," a proud realization of the fact that he is indeed a citizen of the world.

*Afterword*

✽

# TO PARENTS

hor Heyerdahl is a superb role model for all of us, young and old. His courage under fire and refusal to buckle in the face of scathing criticism are virtues that everyone can emulate with pride. He believes what he believes, and he is determined to defend that belief, no matter what.

Thor's life has taken many directions: explorer, writer, archaeologist, lecturer. If there is a single, unifying theme, it is his reverence for nature. Firsthand, he has witnessed the tragic effects of pollution. He knows what will happen unless we start taking better care of this fragile planet.

"Somewhere along the way modern man has gone wrong by failing to acknowledge the huge difference between progress and civilization," he wrote.

As a young man Thor tried to escape "civilization" and failed. And yet in the midst of that failure, he discovered the seeds of a fantastic idea, one that would grow into his life's work.

Like others before him, Thor found the world a rich and wondrous place. Nothing has changed. There are still great adventures out there, just waiting to be discovered. All we need are more fearless explorers like Thor to find them.

# BIBLIOGRAPHY

Heyerdahl, Thor. *The* Kon-Tiki *Expedition*. New York: Allen & Unwin, 1950.

———. *American Indians in the Pacific*. New York: Allen & Unwin, 1952.

———. *Aku-Aku: The Secret of Easter Island*. New York: Allen & Unwin, 1958.

———. *The* Ra *Expeditions*. New York: Allen & Unwin, 1971.

Jacoby, Arnold. *Senor Kon-Tiki*. Chicago: Rand McNally, 1967.

Ralling, Christopher. *The Kon-Tiki Man*. London: BBC Books, 1990.

Steel, Philip. *Thor Heyerdahl and the* Kon-Tiki *Voyage*. Winchester: Zoe Books, 1993.

# GLOSSARY

**balsa.** A very light wood, of the bombax family, found on the west coast of South America and used in model making. It has great buoyancy.

**Berbers.** North African tribe, mainly farmers and nomadic herders, who live in Algeria, Libya, Morocco and Tunisia.

**coral reef.** Made from the external skeletons of marine invertebrates. Jagged to the touch, it is very dangerous for boats.

**diffusionism.** The theory that transmigration among ancient races was far more widespread than is generally believed.

**fjords**. Narrow, deepwater inlets in the Norwegian coastline.

**Long Ears.** Native term for ancient Polynesian settlers, notable for their long earlobes.

**Marquesas.** A chain of mountainous, volcanic islands, situated 740 miles northeast of Tahiti, that are part of Polynesia.

**papyrus.** Stout, reedlike plant, used to make sails, paper, sandals and clothing.

**Polynesia**. A term for many different groups of South Pacific islands.

**prow**. The high bow (front) of a boat.

**sea dog.** An experienced sailor.

**stern**. The rear of a boat.

**Ulysses.** A hero from Greek mythology, renowned as an explorer. The main character in Homer's epic poem, *The Odyssey.*